Ultimate Travel Guide To

Thessaloniki, GREECE

Thessaloniki Uncovered:
The Must-Have Guide
for Every Explorer!

Elizabeth Whyte

COPYRIGHT NOTICE

DISCLAIMER

Please note that the information contained within this document is for educational purposes only. The information contained herein has been obtained from sources believed to be reliable at the time of publication. The opinions expressed herein are subject to change without notice.

Readers acknowledge that the Author / Publisher is not engaging in rendering legal, financial or professional advice. The Publisher / Author disclaims all warranties as to the accuracy, completeness, or adequacy of such information.

The Publisher assumes no liability for errors, omissions, or inadequacies in the information contained herein or from the interpretations thereof. The publisher / Author specifically disclaims any liability from the use or application of the information contained herein or from the interpretations thereof.

TABLE OF CONTENT

Travel and Packing Tips

   What to Bring

   Local Etiquette

   Health and Safety Recommendations

Chapter 2
Exploring Thessaloniki

   Thessaloniki City Overview

How to Get Around in the City

   Public Transportation

   Biking and Walking

   Taxis and Ride-Sharing Services

   Automobile Rentals

Landmarks and Attractions

   The White Tower

   The Archeological Museum

   Rotunda

   Aristotelous Square

   Upper Town (Ano Poli)

   And Many Others...

Excursions and Day Trips

   Halkidiki Peninsula

   Mount Olympus

   Vergina

   Wine Tours

Nightlife and Entertainment

Restaurants and Cuisine

Cafés and Bakeries

Clubs and Bars

Performances and Theaters

Chapter 3
Immersing in Local Culture

History and Heritage

Ancient Thessaloniki

Byzantine and Ottoman Influence

Modern History

Art and Culture

Museums and Galleries

Music and Dance

Festivals and Celebrations

Language and Communication

Greek Expressions

Language Tips

English in Thessaloniki

Shopping and Souvenirs

Markets and Bazaars

Local Products

Bargaining and Shopping Etiquette

Table of Contents

INTRODUCTION

WELCOME TO THESSALONIKI!

I'm thrilled to tell you about my trip to Thessaloniki, Greece, and the unforgettable experiences I had in this dynamic and historic city.

This Ultimate Travel Guide hopes to be your trusted companion as you embark on your adventure in

Thessaloniki. Before we dig into the city's center, let's get a quick rundown of what to expect.

A Brief History of Thessaloniki

Thessaloniki, often known as Salonika or just Thess, is a city that oozes history from every cobblestone. It is Greece's second-largest city and stands ideally along the Thermaic Gulf, offering breathtaking sea views and sunsets.

But Thessaloniki is much more than a scenic setting; it's a place where the past collides with the present, resulting in a distinctive blend of culture, customs, and a lively metropolitan lifestyle.

This city has a long and illustrious history that dates back over two millennia. Cassander, one of Alexander the Great's generals, founded Thessaloniki in 315 BC, and it has witnessed civilizations rise and fall, from the Romans to the Byzantines to the

Ottomans. This historical tapestry is a treasure mine for history aficionados, with its ancient ruins, Byzantine churches, and Ottoman architecture.

Aside from its historical significance, Thessaloniki is also noted for its bustling atmosphere, thriving artistic scene, and diverse culinary offerings. The city is a cultural melting pot, and you can see this in its people, food, and customs.

Thessaloniki has something for everyone, whether you want to explore archaeological sites, eat delectable Greek food, or live the laid-back Mediterranean lifestyle.

Why Go to Thessaloniki?

You may be wondering why you should make Thessaloniki your next travel destination. There are several compelling reasons for this:

Historical Highlights: Thessaloniki is an open-air museum. You may walk through the historic ruins of the Rotunda and the Arch of Galerius, see Byzantine churches like Hagia Sophia, and tour the city's distinctive White Tower.

Rich Cultural Scene: The city's cultural life is vibrant, with theaters, museums, and art galleries. Cultural events abound, from the Thessaloniki International Film Festival to local art shows.

Gastronomic Delights: Greek cuisine is well-known around the world, and Thessaloniki is no exception. The city is a foodie's dream, with tavernas and marketplaces serving wonderful meals like moussaka, souvlaki, and baklava.

Vibrant Nightlife: Nightlife is alive and well in Thessaloniki. The city's nightlife caters to all preferences, whether you choose a peaceful night at a traditional bouzouki bar or dancing till dawn in a lively disco.

Breathtaking Scenery: Beautiful views of the sea abound in the city, and there are numerous local attractions for nature lovers. There is no shortage of natural beauty in Greece, from the lush Halkidiki Peninsula to the magnificent Mount Olympus.

About This Guide

So, what should you expect from this guide? My goal is to provide you with a detailed insider's view of Thessaloniki. I've spent weeks touring the city and immersing myself in its culture, and I want your trip to be as easy and pleasurable as possible.

This book will cover everything from trip planning to local customs, allowing you to make the most of your time in the city.

I'll go over the best times to visit, how to get around the city, must-see attractions, hidden jewels, and a slew of other useful information.

In addition, I'll provide itineraries tailored to your specific interests, whether you're traveling with your family, as a solo traveler, or on a strict budget.

How to Use this Guide

I've structured this guide so that you can easily locate the information you need, whether you're a seasoned traveler or visiting Greece for the first time. Here's how to navigate through it:

Chapter 1: Planning Your Trip: Begin here for important information about when to go, visa requirements, transit alternatives, and lodging. You'll find packing recommendations and safety advice to help you prepare.

Chapter 2: Exploring Thessaloniki: In this section, I'll take you through the city's core, introducing you to its neighborhoods, landmarks, and entertainment options. Whether you're interested in ancient history, modern art, or simply enjoying good food, you'll find it here.

Chapter 3: Immersing in Local Culture: Learn about the history, art, language, and traditions that distinguishes Thessaloniki. I'll assist you in connecting with the locals and developing a greater respect for the city's diverse culture.

Chapter 4: Practical Information: You'll find useful information regarding money, healthcare, safety, and staying connected while in Thessaloniki in this section. When visiting a new place, it is essential to be prepared for any eventuality.

Chapter 5: Itineraries and Travel Tips: You'll find tailored itineraries and advice to make your visit unforgettable, depending on your interests and the length of your stay. There are suggestions for families, lone travelers, foodies, and budget-conscious adventurers.

Chapter 6: Conclusion: Finally, I'll leave you with some closing comments, as well as contact information in case you have any questions or require any assistance during your visit.

So, with this book in hand, prepare to immerse yourself in Thessaloniki's rich history, culture, and vibrant lifestyle.

I hope your trip through this captivating city is as amazing as mine, and that your experiences are memorable and your travels are limitless.

Let's go on this adventure together!

CHAPTER 1

PLANNING YOUR TRIP

It is crucial to plan your trip carefully before commencing your journey to this fascinating destination.

From its rich history and culture to its gorgeous scenery, Thessaloniki has a lot to offer, and the timing of your visit can greatly influence your experience.

So, let us begin the planning process.

When Should You Visit Thessaloniki?

The season is important to consider while deciding when to visit Thessaloniki. Each season provides a different perspective on this Greek treasure.

Seasonal Considerations

Summer (June to August): If you enjoy the sun and the bustling energy of a city in full motion, summer is the season for you. The weather is pleasant, the streets are bustling, and the beaches of the Thermaic Gulf beckon.

There will be plenty of outdoor events and dining options. Expect warmer temperatures as well as the need for sunscreen and swimwear.

Spring (April to May) and Autumn (September to October): Spring and autumn are good for people who want milder temperatures and a quieter ambiance. The city is less crowded than usual, and the weather is ideal for sightseeing and outdoor activities. Whether you're exploring historical buildings or strolling through attractive neighborhoods, the weather and ambiance are ideal.

Winter (November to March): Thessaloniki does not hibernate throughout the winter months. It may be chilly, but it is far from uninteresting. This is an excellent time to discover the city's cultural offerings without the summer throngs.

Furthermore, the adjacent snow-capped mountains provide an extra dimension of grandeur to the landscape. Just remember to bring some extra clothing to keep warm.

Festivals & Events

Thessaloniki is a city that loves to celebrate life, in addition to ancient landmarks and gorgeous scenery. Here are a few significant festivals and events to consider while planning your trip:

Thessaloniki International Film Festival (November): If you enjoy watching movies, November is the month for you. This renowned film festival brings together filmmakers and moviegoers from all over the world to celebrate the art of filmmaking.

Dimitria Festival (October): Visit in October for an excellent cultural experience. The Dimitria Festival is a celebration of arts, music, and culture that highlights the city's thriving cultural environment. It's an excellent time to learn about local customs.

Thessaloniki International Fair (September): Thessaloniki International Fair takes center stage in September. This event is not simply a commercial spectacular, but also a cultural hub. It's a terrific opportunity to learn about the latest developments and products while also experiencing some local culture.

Consider your tastes and interests while organizing your vacation to Thessaloniki. Whether you're a fan of the sun, culture, or winter wonderlands, this city has something for you in every season.

Once you've settled on a season, we can get into the details of preparing your experience in Thessaloniki, Greece.

Entry Requirements and Visas

My flight to Thessaloniki, Greece, was filled with excitement and expectations, but before I could plunge into the wonderful adventures that awaited me, I needed to ensure that all of the essential documentation were in good order.

Visa Details

Visiting Thessaloniki as a Tourist: You're in luck if you're a EU citizen! To visit Thessaloniki and other parts of Greece, all you need is a valid ID card or passport. There is no need for a visa.

Non-EU Citizens: Depending on your nationality, you may be required to obtain a Schengen visa in order to enter Greece.

It is important to confirm the visa requirements for your country with the Greek embassy or consulate. To minimize last-minute headaches, it's generally a good idea to have this settled well in advance of your vacation.

Entry Requirements

It is essential that all of your travel documents be in order. Here are a few things to keep in mind:

Passport Validity: Your passport should be valid for at least six months beyond your intended departure date from Greece. Check the expiration date and, if necessary, renew it.

Customs Regulations: Before you begin packing, become acquainted with the customs regulations. You can bring in a specific number of duty-free commodities, such as tobacco and alcohol. It's a good idea to be aware of the restrictions in order to prevent any customs complications upon arrival.

HOW TO GET TO THESSALONIKI

Now that the documentation is in order, it's time to plan your trip to Thessaloniki and begin your experience.

Transportation Alternatives

Greece is well-connected, and Thessaloniki is easily accessible by numerous modes of transportation. Consider the following options:

International and Domestic Flights

International Flights: Makedonia Airport in Thessaloniki serves as the city's international gateway.

It is roughly 15 kilometers from the city center and has excellent connections to major cities around Europe and the world. During my stay, I came in from Amsterdam, and the flight was quick and easy.

Domestic Flights: If you're already in Greece and want to explore the rest of the nation, domestic flights are a good alternative.

They are especially useful if you are traveling to Thessaloniki from Athens or other Greek cities. The swift flight will get you here quickly, allowing you to begin your experience right away.

The Makedonia Airport has all of the amenities and services that you'd expect from a modern international airport. There are vehicle rental agencies, shops, restaurants, and easy access to public transit, making it straightforward to move from the airport to the city center.

Traveling by Train and Bus

If you want a more breathtaking journey and have the time, riding the train or bus to Thessaloniki can be a rewarding experience. Both are enjoyable and offer stunning views of the Greek countryside.

Train: The train ride from Athens to Thessaloniki is breathtaking, taking you through the heart of Greece.

It's a fantastic opportunity to see more of the nation while also immersing yourself in the culture.

Bus: Another low-cost option for getting to Thessaloniki from other Greek cities is to take the bus. The roads are in good condition, and you may enjoy the beautiful scenery along the way.

Driving to Thessaloniki

Driving to Thessaloniki might be a terrific option for individuals who appreciate the freedom of the open road. Thessaloniki is easily accessible by automobile thanks to Greece's excellent road network.

I drove from Athens to Thessaloniki on my trip, and it was an unforgettable experience. The highways are well-marked, and the journey allows you to see different sections of Greece along the way.

So, whether you like the convenience of air travel, the picturesque routes of trains and buses, or the flexibility of a road trip, Thessaloniki provides a variety of options.

Once you've decided, you'll be on your way to discovering this fascinating city and making great experiences.

Best wishes!

ACCOMMODATION OPTIONS

After I had arranged my tickets and visa, the next exciting stage in my Thessaloniki journey was determining where to stay. Thessaloniki's accommodation options range from magnificent hotels to pleasant budget stays, making it appropriate for all types of travelers.

Hotels and Resorts

Thessaloniki has a wide range of hotels and resorts to suit all interests and budgets. When it comes to these accommodations, here are a few crucial aspects to consider:

City Center Hotels: If you want to be right in the middle of the activity, stay at a city center hotel. These hotels are close to significant attractions, restaurants, and shopping. In addition, you'll most likely have amazing views of the city or the sea.

During my vacation, I stayed in a hotel in the city center, which was ideal for learning about the local culture.

Boutique Hotels: There is a burgeoning boutique hotel scene in Thessaloniki. These smaller, individually owned hotels offer a more personal and intimate experience. You'll often find unique decor and outstanding service. They are ideal for travelers seeking luxury with a personal touch.

Resorts by the Sea: Consider a resort by the shoreline for a more relaxing and beachier feel. The seaside resorts provide stunning sea views as well as a variety of amenities such as pools, restaurants, and easy beach access. They are ideal for those who want to relax and enjoy the Mediterranean atmosphere.

Hostels and Budget Stays

Thessaloniki is not only about luxury; it also welcomes budget-conscious visitors. Here's what to anticipate from hostels and low-cost accommodations:

Hostels: There are some outstanding hostels in Thessaloniki that offer a comfortable and social stay. These are ideal for lone travelers who want to meet like-minded people while staying within their budget. They often organize group events and generate a lively atmosphere.

Guesthouses: There are also cozy guesthouses that provide a genuine Greek experience. These are often family-run businesses that will welcome you with warmth and hospitality. If you want to immerse yourself in the local culture, this is an ideal choice.

Budget Hotels: Consider budget hotels if you want a private room without breaking the bank. They offer simple, comfortable lodging and are ideal for couples or small groups traveling together.

Airbnb and Vacation Rentals

Airbnb and vacation rentals are wonderful options for folks who like a more homey ambiance and extra space. During my stay, I chose an Airbnb, and it was a fantastic experience. Here's what to expect:

Variety of Options: The Airbnb choices in Thessaloniki are varied, ranging from modest apartments in the city center to charming historic houses in the neighborhoods. You can pick a location that meets your preferences and party size.

Explore Thessaloniki Like a Local: Staying in an Airbnb allows you to explore the city like a local. You can prepare your own meals using fresh items from local markets and explore the city at your leisure.

Flexibility: If you like a little more privacy and independence during your stay, Airbnb and vacation rentals allow you to determine your own schedule and completely personalize the space.

Whether you want a luxurious resort, a comfortable guesthouse, a noisy hostel, or a quaint Airbnb, Thessaloniki has lodging to suit every taste and budget.

The goal is to choose the one that best suits your travel style and enriches your entire experience in this amazing city. So, once you've made your decision, you're ready to explore Thessaloniki's delights!

TRAVEL AND PACKING TIPS

Packing for a trip to Thessaloniki, Greece, is an exciting experience. You want to be ready for all of the fantastic things that this city has to offer, and some careful planning can make your journey more comfortable and pleasurable.

What to Bring

Light Clothing: Summers in Thessaloniki may be brutal, so bring lightweight, breathable clothing. Consider shorts, tees, and summer skirts. Remember to bring your swimsuit for beach days!

Layers: If you travel in spring or autumn, temperatures can fluctuate throughout the day. A light jacket or sweater is a smart idea to have on hand for cooler evenings or unexpected weather changes.

Walking Shoes: Thessaloniki is best experienced by foot. You'll be wandering down cobblestone streets and visiting historical buildings, so bring suitable walking shoes.

Sunscreen: Greece is well-known for its sunny weather. To protect yourself from the sun's rays, pack sunscreen, sunglasses, and a wide-brimmed hat.

Adapters: Greece utilizes Type C and Type F power connectors. Don't forget to bring the necessary adapters to keep your gadgets charged.

Travel Documents: Make sure you have your passport, visa (if necessary), travel insurance, and a copy of your itinerary with you. Having these paperwork in order will make your journey go more smoothly.

Daypack: A small daypack is useful for carrying essentials while exploring the city. You may store your water bottle, camera, and other necessities for the day.

Local Etiquette

Greece has a warm and inviting culture, and it is crucial to respect local customs and manners. Here are some things to remember:

Greeks are cordial and usually greet with a kiss on both cheeks. If you're not comfortable with this, a pleasant handshake will suffice.

Dress Code: It is important to dress modestly when visiting churches or monasteries. Both men and women should cover their shoulders and knees. Casual dress is acceptable in other parts of the city.

Tipping: Tipping is customary in Greece. In restaurants, a 10% tip is customary. It is also usual to tip taxi drivers and hotel employees for excellent service.

Public Behavior: Be aware of your actions in public places. While Greeks are generally cordial, loud or disrespectful behavior is considered unpleasant.

Health and Safety Recommendations

Travel Insurance: Travel insurance that covers medical situations is required. Although Greece offers outstanding healthcare services, proper insurance is required for peace of mind.

Stay Hydrated: During the summer, Thessaloniki may get rather hot. Carry a water bottle with you at all times and drink enough of water to stay hydrated, especially if you're touring the city on foot.

Traffic and Roads: Be cautious when crossing the streets in Thessaloniki, as traffic can be heavy. Use marked crosswalks and obey traffic signals at all times.

Emergency Numbers: Learn your local emergency phone numbers. The overall European emergency number is 112, and the emergency numbers in Greece are 100 for police, 166 for medical emergencies, and 199 for the fire service.

Packing for Thessaloniki entails preparing for the city's climate, observing local customs, and guaranteeing your safety and well-being during your visit.

With these packing and travel recommendations, you'll be well-prepared to make the most of your trip to Thessaloniki.

Have a wonderful journey!

CHAPTER 2

EXPLORING THESSALONIKI

I'm excited to guide you through the bustling streets of this interesting city and assist you in navigating its rich cultural tapestry.

In this chapter, we'll look at the city's layout as well as its various districts and neighborhoods, so you know what to expect when you arrive.

Thessaloniki City Overview

Let me give you an overview of this wonderful city before we explore the neighborhoods and districts.

Geographical Layout

Thessaloniki is located on the Thermaic Gulf, overlooking the magnificent seas of the Aegean Sea. Thessaloniki, Greece's second-largest city, is a bustling metropolis with a distinctive geographical layout. Here's a basic rundown:

Waterfront Beauty: The heart of the city beats along the waterfront promenade, where you'll discover a variety of cafes, restaurants, and a breathtaking view of the sea. This is an excellent location for taking in the Mediterranean atmosphere.

Historical Core: The city's historical core is a tangle of narrow alleys teeming with historic structures, lovely squares, and local markets. You'll come across the

White Tower, Thessaloniki's symbol, as well as the historic Roman Rotunda and Arch of Galerius.

Hill of the Castles: The Upper Town, or Ano Poli, is located to the east of the city and features cobblestone lanes, ancient buildings, and the spectacular Trigoniou Tower. It's a journey back in time with stunning views of the city below.

Modern Vibes: The modern part of the city has a dynamic ambiance. Here you'll discover high-end shopping, contemporary art galleries, and a plethora of restaurants serving both Greek and international cuisine.

Districts and Neighborhoods

Thessaloniki is a city of several neighborhoods, each with its own distinct personality and charm. Let's look at some of the most prominent ones:

Ladadika: This historic quarter is well-known for its lively nightlife, which includes various taverns and tavernas. You can also visit art galleries and boutique shops in this area. Ladadika is always busy, and it's a great site to start your Thessaloniki journey.

Kalamaria: A modern and wealthy suburb famed for its lovely coastal promenade, Kalamaria is located along the sea. It's ideal for leisurely strolls, and there are lots of cafes and seafood eateries nearby.

Ano Poli: This is Thessaloniki's hilltop old town. It's a charming tangle of narrow lanes, quaint residences, and historical charm that transports you back in time. For a taste of history, explore the Vlatadon Monastery and the Eptapyrgio Fortress while you're here.

Navarinou Square: If you enjoy street art, this is a must-see. Colorful graffiti adorns the square and surrounding streets, providing a distinct and vivid environment. It also serves as a gathering place for local markets and cultural activities.

Tsimiski Strip: The center of Thessaloniki's contemporary downtown is this lively shopping strip. There are shops, boutiques, cafes, and restaurants all along the street. Tsimiski Street is the place to be whether you enjoy shopping or simply taking in the city's modern vibe.

Peraia: Peraia is a region along the coast famed for its magnificent beaches and seaside tavernas if you're looking for a more casual and beachy environment. It's a great area to relax and enjoy the sun and sea.

Exoches: Exoches is a pleasant suburb with a relaxing outlook, with verdant parks excellent for picnics and leisurely walks. It's a terrific area to get away from the hustle and bustle of the city.

Aretsou: Aretsou is another coastal suburb noted for its marina, where you may take a quiet stroll and enjoy the sea views. It also serves as a hub for seafood restaurants and cafes.

You'll come across a variety of architectural styles, cultures, and flavors as you explore these communities. The diversity of Thessaloniki is part of what makes it such a fascinating and vibrant destination, and I'm confident you'll fall in love with its varied personality.

These areas are only a sliver of what Thessaloniki has to offer. Each has a distinct mood and narrative to tell. The varied neighborhoods of Thessaloniki have something for everyone, whether you're a history buff, a foodie, or simply trying to soak up the Mediterranean sun.

So, let us prepare to explore and discover the city's hidden treasures.

HOW TO GET AROUND IN THE CITY

Getting around Thessaloniki is a breeze, and exploring the city is an adventure in and of itself. Let's go over the various kinds of transportation available that will help you traverse Thessaloniki with ease.

Public Transportation

Thessaloniki has an excellent and reasonably priced public transit system that makes getting around the city a pleasure.

Bus: The city has a well-developed bus network, making it one of the most convenient modes of transportation. Buses run regularly and service a wide range of places, including the city center, neighborhoods, and suburbs. Check out the bus routes and schedules for your destination.

Boat Services: Boat services are available along the waterfront and provide a scenic way to explore the city. These services link the city core to nearby areas and beaches, providing a pleasant and peaceful journey.

Tickets and Cards: Bus tickets can be purchased straight from the driver. There are also daily or multi-day passes available that provide unrestricted travel within a set term. These passes are economical for those who plan to use public transit regularly.

Biking and Walking

Thessaloniki is a very walkable city, thanks to its small size and pedestrian-friendly streets, which make it ideal for exploring on foot.

City Center Strolls: A stroll in the city center is a delight. Walking is the greatest way to discover the narrow alleys, historical landmarks, and welcoming cafes. As you walk around the streets, you'll discover hidden gems and soak in the city's atmosphere.

Biking: The city is developing a biking culture. There are bike rental options available to help you get around the city. Dedicated bike lanes, particularly along the seaside, make cycling both safe and fun.

Taxis and Ride-Sharing Services

Taxis: Taxis are often available in Thessaloniki and provide a simple way to get around, particularly if you're going to locations that are not easily accessible by public transportation. Use licensed taxis and inquire about the approximate fee before beginning your journey.

Ride-Sharing Applications: Ride-sharing applications are becoming increasingly popular in Thessaloniki. They provide an alternative to traditional taxis and can be a more cost-effective solution. It's useful for visitors searching for a quick and easy way to get around the city.

Automobile Rentals

Car rentals are readily available in Thessaloniki if you prefer the flexibility and independence of driving.

Exploration Freedom: Renting a car allows you to visit neighboring attractions and explore the surrounding areas at your own time. For a day excursion, you can easily reach areas like Halkidiki's stunning beaches or Mount Olympus.

Procedure for Renting an Automobile: The procedure for renting an automobile is simple. Various international and local rental businesses provide a diverse selection of vehicles, allowing you to select one that meets your demands and budget.

While each form of transportation in Thessaloniki has merits, combining them can provide a well-rounded experience of the city. Whether you want to walk through the historical center, take a bus to a specific location, or enjoy the convenience of a cab ride, Thessaloniki's transportation options cater to a wide range of interests and guarantee that you make the most of your time in this great city.

LANDMARKS AND ATTRACTIONS

Thessaloniki is a city rich in history and culture, with a plethora of amazing landmarks and attractions just waiting to be explored.

Allow me to take you on a virtual tour of some of the must-see attractions that I had the pleasure of seeing during my time in this enthralling city.

The White Tower

The majestic White Tower is unquestionably Thessaloniki's most recognizable symbol. It boldly stands along the waterfront, providing a lovely backdrop against the sea. This cylindrical tower has had a turbulent history, having served as a fortress, a prison, and now a museum.

The panoramic view from the top is spectacular, offering a breathtaking perspective over the city and the Thermaic Gulf. The museum within provides an in-depth look into Thessaloniki's history, making it a must-see sight.

The Archeological Museum

The Archaeological Museum of Thessaloniki is a must-see for history buffs. It houses an extraordinary collection of artifacts spanning centuries, illustrating the region's history from prehistoric origins to the Roman and Byzantine eras.

The exhibition has been expertly curated, with gorgeous sculptures, exquisite mosaics, and relics that shed light on the city's rich history on display. It's like going back in time and discovering Thessaloniki's history over the years.

Rotunda

The Rotunda is an architectural marvel that was originally intended as a mausoleum for Roman Emperor Galerius but was later converted into a Christian church and, eventually, a mosque.

Its vast size and eye-catching architecture make it a sight to behold. Inside, exquisite mosaics decorate the walls, providing an insight into the building's rich history. The Rotunda is a fascinating blend of architectural forms and a tribute to the city's eclectic heritage.

Aristotelous Square

Aristotelous Square is Thessaloniki's beating heart, a vibrant meeting place surrounded by cafes, shops, and antique buildings. The square is a dynamic hub where locals and tourists congregate to relax, people-watch, and absorb the vitality of the city.

The magnificence of the square's neoclassical buildings is simply impressive. This area is an essential stop for experiencing the pulse of the city, whether taking a leisurely stroll or having a coffee at one of the many outdoor cafes.

Upper Town (Ano Poli)

Ano Poli, or the Upper Town, is a lovely region tucked on the hill above the city that transports you back in time. Walking down its cobblestone streets, you'll come across traditional residences, ancient churches, and a peaceful ambiance.

Perched on a hillside, the Vlatadon Monastery provides a serene retreat as well as an insight into the city's religious history. The view from Ano Poli is spectacular, with panoramic views of Thessaloniki and the Mediterranean beyond.

And Many Others...

Thessaloniki never ceases to amaze with its wealth of attractions:

Arch of Galerius: The Arch of Galerius is a spectacular triumphal arch that serves as a reminder of the city's Roman past. Its magnificent carvings and historical significance make it a must-see.

Church of Agios Dimitrios: Dedicated to the city's patron saint, this large church is a stunning example of Byzantine architecture. Its historical, artistic, and religious significance make it an important component of Thessaloniki's heritage.

Museums Abound: Thessaloniki is home to numerous museums, including the Museum of Byzantine Culture, the Museum of Photography, and the Museum of the Macedonian Struggle, all of which provide unique insights into the city's complex history and cultural richness.

Modiano Market and Kapani Market: These vibrant markets are a sensory delight. Explore the small streets where residents sell fresh fruit, aromatic spices, and a range of goods, providing a true experience of Thessaloniki life.

Navarinou Square and Street Art: For art lovers, Navarinou Square is a refuge of brilliant street art, with colorful murals decorating buildings and walls, creating an open-air gallery worth exploring.

Hagia Sophia: Unlike its Istanbul counterpart, Thessaloniki's Hagia Sophia is an ancient church with exquisite mosaics and a rich history.

Toumba Stadium: Catching a game at Toumba Stadium, home of PAOK FC, provides an insight into the city's enthusiastic sports culture.

Attractions in Thessaloniki reflect the city's unique history and the mix of cultures that have left their mark on this vibrant metropolis.

Each site has a distinct tale, allowing visitors to piece together the city's past and present while displaying the tapestry of Thessaloniki's legacy.

There's always something new and fascinating to discover around every turn in this city, making it a treasure for history, culture, and adventure seekers.

EXCURSIONS AND DAY TRIPS

While Thessaloniki city is a cultural and historical treasure trove, the neighboring areas offer a world of discovery. Let's have a look at some of the most appealing day trips and excursions I had the pleasure of experiencing while in Thessaloniki.

Halkidiki Peninsula

The Halkidiki Peninsula, just a short distance from Thessaloniki, is a sanctuary of clean beaches and verdant surroundings. This breathtaking location is divided between three peninsulas: Kassandra, Sithonia, and Athos, each with its own distinct appeal.

Kassandra: Known for its bustling beach resorts and dynamic nightlife, Kassandra is ideal for sunbathers and partygoers. I went on a day trip to Sani Beach, which had golden dunes and crystal-clear waves, and it was an idyllic location for leisure.

Sithonia: Sithonia is a more relaxed and nature-focused location with calm beaches and isolated coves. It seemed like walking into a postcard when I explored the isolated Orange Beach, where the azure sea met the pine-clad rocks.

Mount Athos: Mount Athos is a UNESCO World Heritage site and an extraordinary spiritual destination.

While women are not permitted to join the monastic state, I had the opportunity to take a boat excursion down Mount Athos' coast, marveling at the monasteries located on towering cliffs.

Halkidiki is an excellent day trip location, offering a unique combination of relaxation, adventure, and culture, all within a short drive of Thessaloniki.

Mount Olympus

My day trip to Mount Olympus was one of the highlights of my stay in Thessaloniki. This spectacular summit, known as the "Mountain of the Gods" in Greek mythology, offers more than simply amazing hiking options.

I traveled to Litochoro, the entryway to Olympus, and went on a hike that allowed me to enjoy the pristine landscape and breathtaking views.

Hiking Paths: There are numerous hiking paths available for people of all experience levels. The Enipeas Gorge trail is easily accessible and provides a beautiful route along the Enipeas River that leads to the picturesque Prionia area.

Scenic Views: As you ascend higher, the views become more breathtaking. I was rewarded with breathtaking views of the Thermaic Gulf and the Aegean Sea as I climbed the peak. A photographer's dream has come true.

Mythical Connection: Knowing you're walking in the footsteps of the ancient Greek gods is a surreal and mysterious experience. The summit, Mytikas, is Greece's highest point and a goal for many hikers.

Vergina

Vergina, a UNESCO World Heritage site, is an archeological marvel that offers insight into Macedonia's regal history. It's only a short drive from Thessaloniki and makes for an excellent day excursion for history aficionados.

The Royal Tombs: The Royal Tombs are the ultimate burial place of King Philip II, father of Alexander the Great, and other members of the royal family. The exquisite paintings and valuables contained within these tombs are breathtaking.

Museum of the Royal Tombs: Adjacent to the tombs, the museum contains an impressive collection of objects unearthed at the site. These relics provide a clear knowledge of ancient Macedonian culture and its relationship with Greece.

The Palace of Aigai: Explore the ruins of the ancient city of Aigai, which served as the Kingdom of Macedon's first capital. The city has an agora, a theater, and other structures that provide insight into everyday life in antiquity.

Wine Tours

Northern Greece's wine area is an oenophile's dream, and it's only a short drive from Thessaloniki. I went on a wine tour to see the vineyards, learn about winemaking, and, of course, drink some excellent Greek wines.

Winery Tours: Visiting wineries in Naoussa and Drama was a joy. The trips included vineyard strolls, guided tastings of local wines, and insights into the winemaking process.

Local Grape Varietals: I discovered rare Greek grape varietals such as Xinomavro, Assyrtiko, and Agiorgitiko. These wines are not only delicious, but they also reflect the terroir of the region.

Beautiful Landscapes: The wine areas are surrounded by beautiful scenery, including rolling vine-covered hills and lovely winemaking estates. It's an excellent opportunity to explore the Greek countryside.

Thessaloniki is a fantastic starting point for these incredible day adventures, providing a well-rounded experience of Greece's natural beauty, historical riches, and culinary delights. Whether you're interested in the sea, mountains, antiquities, or wine, the city offers a plethora of possibilities for creating fantastic day trips and excursions.

NIGHTLIFE AND ENTERTAINMENT

The bustling entertainment scene in Thessaloniki is one of its most intriguing aspects. From delectable culinary experiences to busy nightlife and cultural shows, the city never fails to provide a diverse range of entertainment alternatives to suit everyone's tastes.

Restaurants and Cuisine

The gastronomic scene of Thessaloniki is a trip through exquisite Greek flavors and cosmopolitan influences. The city has it all of it, whether you're a foodie looking for local delicacies or desiring exotic cuisines.

Traditional Tavernas: It is essential to visit traditional tavernas. These intimate cafés provide classic Greek delicacies like moussaka, souvlaki, and a variety of mezedes (small plates) that highlight Greece's rich flavors. Ano Poli, Ladadika, and the city center are brimming with lovely tavernas serving delectable cuisine.

Seafood and Fish Tavernas: As a coastline city, Thessaloniki has plentiful supply of fresh fish. Restaurants near the waterfront serve the day's catch, allowing you to sample the flavors of the Aegean Sea.

International Cuisine: From Italian and Asian to Middle Eastern and beyond, the city's global culture shines through in its diversified restaurant scene. For those looking for a flavor of home or a new culinary adventure, there are wonderful international restaurants serving a variety of cuisines.

Cafés and Bakeries

Greek Coffee Culture: The café culture of Thessaloniki is an important element of the city's social fabric. Cafes, known as kafenia, are perfect places to unwind, sip a Greek coffee, and people-watch. The aromas of freshly made coffee floating through the air enhance the experience.

Bakeries and Sweets: Satisfy your sweet craving at the city's bakeries, which provide a variety of delectable delicacies and pastries. You must taste the famed bougatsa, a delectable pastry filled with cream or cheese, as well as the syrup-soaked baklava.

Cafes with a View: Head to cafes with rooftop terraces along the waterfront for a beautiful view of the city. It's a peaceful experience to sip a frappe or an espresso while watching the sunset or the city lights twinkle.

Clubs and Bars

The nightlife in Thessaloniki is as broad as it is lively, with a variety of choices for a fun-filled evening.

Bars and Cocktail Lounges: There are numerous stylish bars and cocktail lounges in the city. There's something for everyone, whether you like a more relaxed atmosphere or a more active atmosphere. I had beverages at chic bars in Ladadika and the city center.

Nightclubs and Music Venues: After dark, the city comes alive with throbbing nightclubs and live music venues. The music industry caters to a wide range of preferences, from mainstream favorites to alternative sounds, assuring a memorable night out for music fans.

Open-Air Pubs and Terraces: During the summer, open-air pubs and terraces become popular hangouts.

These outdoor settings provide a pleasant atmosphere, ideal for relaxing with friends beneath the stars.

Performances and Theaters

Theatre Performances: Thessaloniki has a thriving theater culture, with a variety of theaters providing plays, musicals, and performances for a wide range of people. It's an excellent approach to become acquainted with the local arts and culture scene.

Cultural Events: Be on the lookout for cultural events, festivals, and live performances taking place throughout the city. There's always something going on in Thessaloniki, from music festivals to art exhibitions and dance performances.

Concerts and Live Music: The city hosts a variety of concerts and live music events showcasing both local and international musicians. There's a concert for everyone, whether you like classical music, rock, jazz, or traditional Greek music.

The entertainment and nightlife scene in Thessaloniki is diversified and energetic, catering to a wide range of interests.

Whether you're a foodie eager to sample local fare, a night owl searching for a dynamic nightlife, or a culture buff interested in shows and art, this city boasts an unlimited choice of entertainment to keep your evenings as lively or serene as you like.

CHAPTER 3

IMMERSING IN LOCAL CULTURE

The rich tapestry of Thessaloniki's culture - a mash-up of historical, artistic, and local traditions has weaved themselves together over time.

Join me on this tour through the layers of history, art, and cultural vibrancy that make up this great city.

History and Heritage

Thessaloniki is a historical treasure trove, with roots dating back to ancient times. Each epoch has left an unmistakable imprint on the city's unique heritage.

Ancient Thessaloniki

Thessaloniki, founded in 315 BC by Cassander, a general of Alexander the Great, has a particular historical significance. The city was named after Cassander's wife, Thessalonike, and swiftly rose to prominence as an important port and trade center in the Roman and Byzantine empires.

Archaeological Remains: The ruins of the ancient city can be seen in a variety of locations, including the Roman Agora, a historic market square where traders formerly congregated. The Palace of Galerius and the Arch of Galerius are also relics of the city's Roman influence.

Byzantine and Ottoman Influence

Byzantine Legacy: The history of Thessaloniki is inextricably linked to the Byzantine Empire. The city thrived under Byzantine authority, resulting in the construction of numerous magnificent churches and monasteries.

The Church of Agios Dimitrios, devoted to the city's patron saint, is an excellent example of Byzantine architecture and art.

Ottoman Presence: Ottoman dominance shaped the city's history, affecting its culture and architecture. The Ottoman influence may be seen in the Bey Hamam, an antique Ottoman bathhouse, and the Hamza Bey Mosque, which has been converted into an exhibition space.

Modern History

Events of the 20th Century: Thessaloniki has seen its fair share of modern historical events. The city was important in the Balkan Wars and the Greco-Turkish War.

The Great Fire of 1917 destroyed a large portion of the city, prompting restoration of Thessaloniki, which resulted in the development of new neighborhoods and modern architecture.

Influence of Refugees and Diaspora: Following the population exchange after World War I and the inflow of refugees from Asia Minor, Thessaloniki experienced an influx of many cultures, contributing to its cosmopolitan aspect.

Today, the city's population and cultural variety reflect this.

ART AND CULTURE

Thessaloniki is an art and culture haven, with a thriving artistic environment that values both inventiveness and heritage.

Museums and Galleries

The Museum of Byzantine Culture is a treasure trove of Byzantine relics, including religious icons, frescoes, and other artistic works. It gives a thorough understanding of the Byzantine era and its impact on the city's culture.

Archaeological Museum: A must-see for history buffs, this museum displays a variety of relics and sculptures spanning ages, illuminating the region's history from prehistoric times to the Roman era.

Teloglion Foundation of Art: This art gallery showcases contemporary works of art, displaying Thessaloniki's modern artistic expressions and inventiveness.

Music and Dance

Traditional Music and Dance: Traditional music and dance abound in the city. Greek folk music and dance events, such as the Bouzoukia, provide an authentic taste of Greek culture.

Live Music: You may catch live music performances ranging from classical to modern in a variety of venues throughout the city. Concert halls, theaters, and outdoor events provide a wide range of musical experiences.

Festivals and Celebrations

Thessaloniki International Film Festival: This renowned festival honors cinema and brings filmmakers and film aficionados from all over the world together.

Dimitria Festival: A celebration of arts and culture, this festival features a range of events across the city, including music, theater, and dance performances.

Cultural Festivities: Throughout the year, a variety of cultural events and festivities display the city's unique spirit and provide insight into local traditions and customs.

The cultural landscape in Thessaloniki is a living monument to the city's rich history, artistic expression, and ongoing appreciation of traditions.

Every facet of its culture, from ancient inspirations to modern manifestations, contributes to the city's charm, making it an enticing destination for visitors looking to immerse themselves in a tapestry of history, art, and local traditions.

LANGUAGE AND COMMUNICATION

Understanding the local language and communication norms can substantially increase your experience when visiting a new destination like Thessaloniki, allowing for better interaction with the friendly residents.

Greek Expressions

Greetings and Politeness: Learning a few basic Greek phrases can open numerous possibilities. "Kalimera" is Greek for "good morning," "Kalispera" is Greek for "good evening," and "Efharisto" is Greek for "thank you."

The Greeks appreciate people who try to communicate in their language, even if it's just a simple "Yasou" for "hello."

Simple Conversational Phrases: In everyday conversations, phrases like "Parakalo" for "please" and "Signomi" for "excuse me" can go a long way. "Poso kani afto?" which translates to "How much is this?" may come in handy on shopping trips.

Menu Navigation: Familiarizing yourself with food-related terminology might make your eating experience more enjoyable. "Mou aresi auto" means "I like this," which is ideal for savoring local cuisine, whereas "Den troo kreas" implies "I don't eat meat" if you have dietary restrictions.

Language Tips

While many people understand English, knowing some basic Greek words can be really useful. Carry a small phrasebook or use language learning applications to help you communicate with the locals.

Pronunciation and Accent: Greek pronunciation may differ from what you're used to, so practice and become acquainted with the accent. Locals will appreciate your efforts, even if they aren't flawless.

Body Language and Hand Gestures: Greeks are expressive and often use hand gestures to accentuate or convey feelings. Understanding the intricacies of their body language can help you communicate more effectively.

English in Thessaloniki

English Proficiency: Many natives in Thessaloniki, particularly those in the tourism and hospitality industries, speak English fluently. You'll notice that younger generations speak English more fluently, making it easier to communicate in areas like hotels, restaurants, and tourist sites.

Multilingual Signs and Menus: Signs and menus in both Greek and English are common in prominent locations and tourist destinations. However, at more local or traditional establishments, they may be exclusively in Greek, making deciphering them an authentic experience.

Patience and understanding: While English is often spoken, particularly in tourist regions, demonstrating patience and understanding when there is a language barrier can go a long way. Simple sentences and gestures can quickly bridge the communication gap.

SHOPPING AND SOUVENIRS

Shopping in Thessaloniki is a fascinating experience, with a wide range of unique products and cultural treasures on offer.

Markets and Bazaars

Modiano and Kapani Markets: These vibrant markets offer a genuine experience of local life. Stroll through the small lanes and bustling kiosks where sellers sell fresh produce, aromatic spices, and regional delicacies.

To take up the ambiance, embrace the rush of activity and mingle with the sellers.

Bezesteni Market: This covered bazaar sells traditional crafts, jewelry, and gifts. You'll find handcrafted products and one-of-a-kind pieces that make fantastic souvenirs of your journey.

Local Products

Olive Oil and Olives: Greece is well-known for its high-quality olive oil and a variety of olive varieties. Many shops and markets sell a variety of local olive oils that are ideal for gifting or personal use.

Honey and Sweets: The country's honey is well-known for its flavor and health advantages. To satiate your sweet tooth, look for local thyme honey and other desserts such as loukoumi (Greek delight) or baklava.

Wine and Spirits: Greece's wine business is thriving. As a souvenir, buy a bottle of local wine, such as a strong red Xinomavro or a crisp white Assyrtiko.

Bargaining and Shopping Etiquette

Bargaining is not typical in official stores or supermarkets, but it is accepted in marketplaces and smaller retailers. Approach it with courtesy and respect. You may not always receive a better deal, but it's worth a shot.

Respect Local Customs: It important to be polite and considerate when shopping. Take your time, relax, and strike up a polite chat with the shops. Taking an interest in their items often ends in a more enjoyable shopping experience.

Cultural Sensitivity: It is polite to obtain permission before photographing the sellers or their products in markets or businesses. Some may decline, so always respect their wishes.

The language and shopping experiences in Thessaloniki are a fantastic opportunity to immerse yourself in the local culture.

Whether it's learning Greek words to communicate with locals or discovering unique products in vibrant markets, these factors enrich your experience and allow you to enjoy the city's traditions while creating lasting memories of your stay in Thessaloniki.

CHAPTER 4

PRACTICAL INFORMATION

Keeping the practicalities in mind when touring Thessaloniki is essential for a pleasant and memorable trip.

These details play a key role in making your vacation experience hassle-free, from managing cash to ensuring safety and remaining connected.

Currency and Money Exchange

Euro (€): Greece's official currency is the euro. To handle transactions more easily, become acquainted with euro denominations. The euro banknotes are available in the following denominations: €5, €10, €20, €50, €100, €200, and €500.

Euros are also divided into cents. Coins are available in denominations of 1, 2, 5, 10, 20, and 50 cents, as well as €1 and €2.

Banking and ATM

ATMs & Withdrawals: ATMs are widely available in Thessaloniki, particularly in commercial districts, airports, and near important tourist attractions. All major credit and debit cards are accepted. However, it is advisable to notify your bank of your vacation plans in order to avoid any unforeseen card complications.

Banking Hours: Banks in Thessaloniki are typically open from 8:00 a.m. to 2:00 p.m., Monday through Friday. On some days, some branches may have extended hours.

Currency Exchange: While currency exchange offices are available, they may not provide the best prices. It's easier to withdraw money from ATMs, where you'll get a good exchange rate.

Medical and Health Services

Hospitals and Clinics: Thessaloniki has contemporary medical facilities and hospitals staffed by highly skilled medical personnel. Public hospitals provide emergency services, while private clinics are also available for medical aid.

Pharmacies: Pharmacies, denoted by a green cross, are conveniently located around the city. They normally have set hours of operation, but there is always one that is available 24 hours a day, seven days a week for emergencies.

Travel Insurance

The Importance of Travel Insurance: Before your vacation, consider purchasing comprehensive travel insurance.

It serves as a safety net in the event of an unanticipated medical emergency, trip cancellation, misplaced luggage, or other unforeseen occurrence. Check your policy to be sure it covers all of your travel requirements.

Insurance Coverage: Before departing, evaluate your insurance policy to determine what it covers and whether it applies to overseas travel. Make certain that it includes medical coverage, including emergency evacuation if needed.

Safety and Emergency Contacts

Emergency Contact Number: In Greece, dial 112 for rapid assistance in an emergency. This number provides access to police, fire, and ambulance services.

Tourist Police: There are tourist police in Thessaloniki who can aid tourists in the event of theft, misplaced items, or other non-emergency issues. They're prevalent in tourist destinations and important transportation hubs.

Consulates and Embassies

Embassy Contact Information: It's a good idea to know your country's embassy or consulate's contact information in case you need assistance, such as lost passports or legal issues.

Location and Contact Information: In emergency cases, your embassy or consulate can assist you. Locating the nearest embassy or consulate upon arrival can be a proactive approach for most travelers.

Internet and communication

Local SIM Cards: Getting a local SIM card can be a cheap way to stay connected. SIM cards from major providers such as Cosmote, Vodafone, and Wind are available in kiosks and phone shops.

Mobile Data Plans: There are various data plans available, each with a different amount of data and validity period. These plans are often low-cost and allow you to stay connected throughout your journey.

Wi-Fi Accessibility

Many hotels, cafes, restaurants, and public locations in Thessaloniki have free Wi-Fi. It is usual for restaurants and public venues to give internet connectivity.

Internet Cafes: Although they are becoming less common, internet cafes still exist in some areas of the city, offering computers and internet connection for a fee.

Taking care of the details is vital for a stress-free travel experience. Being knowledgeable about currency, healthcare, safety, and communication alternatives allows you to focus on the beauty and experiences that Thessaloniki has to offer.

SAMPLE ITINERARY

Whether you're here for a short visit or a prolonged one, experiencing Thessaloniki necessitates a carefully designed plan. Here are some well-planned itineraries and travel suggestions to help you make the most of your time in this enthralling city.

One-Week Itinerary

A week in Thessaloniki provides a healthy combination of historical sightseeing, cultural encounters, and a taste of the city's bustling culture.

Day One: Arrival and City Tour

Arrive in the morning and settle into your lodging.

Afternoon: Begin with a stroll in the city center. Aristotelous Square, the Arch of Galerius, and the Rotunda are all worth seeing.

Evening: Try your first Greek meal at a local taverna in the Ladadika area.

Day 2: Historical Exploration

Morning: Begin your day with Thessaloniki's famed White Tower. Climb to the peak for spectacular views.

In the afternoon, pay a visit to the Archaeological Museum, which houses an extraordinary collection of relics.

Evening: Take a stroll down the waterfront to enjoy the sunset and waterfront eateries.

Day 3: Ano Poli and Byzantine Heritage

Explore Ano Poli, the Upper Town, in the morning. Visit the Agios Dimitrios Church and the Trigoniou Tower.

Afternoon: Stroll along the cobblestone streets and take in the stunning city views.

Evening: Dine in a typical Greek taverna in the Ano Poli neighborhood.

Day 4: Market Visit and Shopping

Morning: Visit Modiano and Kapani Markets to immerse yourself in local culture. Try some of the local vegetables and delights.

Afternoon: Browse the Bezesteni Market for one-of-a-kind souvenirs and gifts.

Evening: Unwind in a cafe with some Greek sweets.

Day 5: Halkidiki Day Trip

Morning: Visit the Halkidiki Peninsula's beautiful beaches and villages.

Afternoon: Swim, sunbathe, or participate in water activities.

Evening: Dine on seafood at a coastal taverna.

Day 6: Museum and Cultural Activities

Morning: Learn about the city's history at the Museum of Byzantine Culture.

Afternoon: Visit the Teloglion Foundation of Art to see exhibitions of modern art.

Evening: See a show at a local theater or concert hall.

Day 7: Rest and Exploration

Morning: Take a stroll down the city's promenade.

Afternoon: Look for hidden jewels or return to old haunts.

Evening: Treat yourself to a goodbye dinner at a rooftop restaurant.

Two-Week Itinerary

A two-week stay in Thessaloniki provides for a more in-depth tour of the city as well as the opportunity to go on fascinating day trips to adjacent sites.

(Days 1–7): Stick to the one-week itinerary.

Day 8: Mount Olympus Excursion

Take a day excursion to Mount Olympus for trekking and breathtaking views of nature.

Days 9-10: Vergina and Wine Tours

Explore ancient royal tombs in Vergina.

Participate in wine tours and tastings in local wine areas.

Days 11-14: Flexible Days

Use this time to explore Thessaloniki further or to do additional day trips based on personal interests.

Consider exploring more of Halkidiki, visiting more distant settlements, or simply strolling through the city's hidden corners at your leisure.

Travel Tips for Families

Attractions for Children: Waterland Water Park and the Thessaloniki Science Center & Technology Museum provide entertaining activities for children.

Family-friendly Accommodations: Accommodations near parks or in family-friendly communities are ideal for families traveling with children.

Cultural Activities: Involve the entire family in cultural activities such as visiting museums or watching open-air performances appropriate for all ages.

Travel Tips for Solo Travelers

Stay in Central Areas: For convenience, choose lodgings in the city center or near major attractions.

Participate in Tours or Workshops: Attend city tours, cooking lessons, or cultural workshops to meet other visitors and locals.

Precautions for Safety: Be cautious, especially at night, and avoid poorly lit or secluded areas.

Travel Tips for Food Enthusiasts

Local Food Tours: Take a food tour to sample a range of local meals and learn about their preparation.

Local Markets: Visit Modiano and Kapani markets to sample authentic Greek goods and delicacies.

Cooking Classes: Enroll in a cooking class to understand the mysteries of Greek food and flavors.

Travel Tips for Budget Travelers

Accommodation Options: For a low-cost stay, consider hostels, guesthouses, or Airbnb.

Local Eateries: For economical yet delicious meals, visit local tavernas and smaller restaurants.

Free Attractions: To get a feel for Thessaloniki, visit free attractions such as as parks, churches, and city squares.

Making the most of your time in Thessaloniki requires balancing sightseeing, immersion in local culture, and practical considerations.

Whether you're traveling with family, alone, on a budget, or as a foodie, these itineraries and advice will make your trip pleasurable and memorable.

CHAPTER 5

CONCLUSION

As my time in Thessaloniki comes to an end, I think on the fascinating experiences, cultural surprises, and captivating charm that this city has to offer.

Allow me to distill the essence of the ultimate experience in Thessaloniki.

Your Ultimate Thessaloniki Experience

Rich Historical Tapestry: Thessaloniki is a historical treasure trove, with relics of ancient civilizations mixed with Byzantine and Ottoman influences.

Exploring its ancient landmarks such as the White Tower, Archaeological Museum, and Ano Poli feels like going back in time.

Cultural Immersion: From lively festivals to contemporary art galleries, Thessaloniki is a cultural melting pot. Understanding the city's pulse requires embracing local customs, eating traditional cuisine, and attending music or theatrical performances.

Warm Hospitality: The people's hospitality is unparalleled. Engaging with people, learning a few Greek words, and enjoying their gastronomic pleasures adds to the experience.

Beautiful Scenery: The city's geography is breathtaking. Its proximity to the sea, attractive neighborhoods, and scenic views provide a tranquil yet bustling atmosphere.

Hidden Gems and Day Trips: Thessaloniki offers more than just the metropolis. Day visits to the beaches of Halkidiki or the historical site of Vergina reveal even more of Greece's splendor.

Feedback and Additional Assistance

Your feedback is crucial in refining and improving the experiences of future tourists. Here's how you can convey your insights:

Online Evaluations: To assist other tourists, consider leaving reviews on platforms such as TripAdvisor, Google Reviews, or booking websites.

Direct Communication: If you have detailed feedback or suggestions, reaching out out to travel forums or the guide's publisher directly may help to enhance future editions.

Other Resources

Further Reading: Look for extra resources in Thessaloniki, such as travel blogs, novels, or films. They provide a variety of viewpoints and insights on the city's culture and history.

Local Assistance: Even after your stay, use local tourism information centers or city guides for further information, tips, and fresh discoveries.

As my time in Thessaloniki comes to an end, I depart with a heart full of memories and a mind enhanced by this magnificent city's colorful tapestry. Thessaloniki is more than a destination; it's an engaging experience that leaves an imprint on your heart and begs you to return.

This city has made an unforgettable imprint on my travels with its history, culture, and amiable embrace.

TOOLS AND RESOURCES

As I bid farewell to the wonderful city of Thessaloniki, I believe it is of the utmost importance to provide valuable tools and information to fellow tourists in order to enhance their experience in this remarkable place.

Important Phrases and Vocabulary

Learning a few Greek phrases can enhance your visit to Thessaloniki by making interactions with locals more enjoyable and meaningful. Here are some key terms and phrases that I found quite helpful during my stay:

Polite Expressions and Greetings:

- "Kalimera" (Καλημέρα) - Good morning
- "Kalispera" (Καλησπέρα) - Good evening
- "Yasou" (Γειά σου) - Hello
- "Efharisto" (Ευχαριστώ) - Thank you
- "Parakalo" (Παρακαλώ) - Please

Basic Dining and Food Terms:

- "Fagito" (Φαγητό) - Food
- "Psomi" (Ψωμί) - Bread
- "Krasí" (Κρασί) - Wine
- "Ouzo" (Ούζο) - Traditional Greek alcoholic drink
- "Menu" (Μενού) - Menu

Navigational Phrases:

- "Thalassa" (Θάλασσα) - Sea
- "Pou einai i Paralia?" (Πού είναι η παραλία;) - Where is the beach?
- "Odoiporikó" (Οδοιπορικό) - Travel guide
- "Anikse to parathiro, parakalo" (Ανοίξε το παράθυρο, παρακαλώ) - Open the window, please

While just a few samples of the Greek language, these phrases can considerably enhance your interactions and experiences while visiting the city.

Reading Lists and Resources

Here are some resources that I found quite useful during my stay in Thessaloniki to delve deeper into the rich tapestry of the city's history, culture, and other areas of interest:

Rick Steves' "Pocket Athens & the Peloponnese" is a great travel companions, providing helpful insights, practical recommendations, and maps.

Historical Books: Mark Mazower's "Thessaloniki: City of Ghosts" and "Salonica, City of Ghosts" provide an in-depth overview of the city's complex past, from antiquity to the present.

Culinary Exploration: Learn about the flavors of Greece by reading cookbooks like "Vefa's Kitchen" by Vefa Alexiadou, which has real Greek recipes and culinary inspirations.

These materials contain a variety of information that can help you better comprehend Thessaloniki's culture, history, and culinary legacy. These items can enhance your trip in Thessaloniki, whether you're looking for historical insights, local gastronomy exploration, or simply practical travel advice.

Throughout my trips, I've learned to appreciate the value of these linguistic tools and perceptive resources, which have greatly enriched my understanding of this magnificent city.

My aim is that they will serve you equally well, guiding you through Thessaloniki's rich tapestry of offerings and delivering a wonderful and culturally stimulating travel experience.

Printed in Great Britain
by Amazon

46154656R00059